W9-APJ-846

A Child's
Garden of Verses

HAPPY THOUGHT

The world is so full of a number of things,
I'm sure we should all be as happy as kings.

A DK PUBLISHING BOOK

Poems and paintings selected by Miriam Farbey and Chris Fraser
Designers Peter Fickling, Chris Fraser • **Line drawings** Jenny Thorne
Picture Research Jo Walton, Louise Thomas • **Production** Katy Holmes
DTP Designer Kim Browne

First American Edition, 1997
2 4 6 8 10 9 7 5 3
Published in the United States by DK Publishing, Inc.
95 Madison Avenue New York, New York 10016
Visit us on the World Wide Web at http://www.dk.com
Copyright © 1997 Dorling Kindersley Limited
All rights reserved. No part of this publication may be reproduced, stored in a retrieval system,
or transmitted in any form or by any means, electronic, mechanical, photocopying, recording,
or otherwise, without the prior written permission of the copyright owner.
A catalog record for this book is available from the Library of Congress.
Published in Great Britain by Dorling Kindersley Ltd.
ISBN 0 7894-2068-6
Color reproduction by GRB graphica, Verona
Printed and bound by Tien Wah Press in Singapore

The publisher would like to thank the following for their kind permission to reproduce the photographs:

The Art Institute of Chicago: Claude Monet, French, 1840–1926, *The Artist's House at Argenteuil (La Maison de l'artist à Argenteuil)*, oil on canvas, 1873, 60.2 x 73.3 cm, Mr. and Mrs. Martin A. Ryerson Collection, 1933.1153 photograph © 1996, All Rights Reserved 31.
Bridgeman Art Library, London: Whitford and Hughs, London 7, 17; Ackermann and Johnson Ltd., London 9; Graphische Sammlung Albertina, Vienna 11; Bradford Art Galleries and Museums 13; Laurence Pollinger Limited and the Estate of Mrs. J. C. Robinson 15; Private Collection 19, 25; City of Bristol Museum and Art Gallery 21; Christopher Wood Gallery, London 27; National Museum, Stockholm 29.
Sotheby's Picture Library, London: 23.
Jacket: **Tate Gallery, London**: *Carnation Lily Lily Rose* John Singer Sargent, front c; **Bridgeman Art Library, London**: Private Collection, inside front tc; Whitford and Hughs, London, Back c;
Mary Evans Picture Library: inside back tc.

A Child's
Garden of Verses

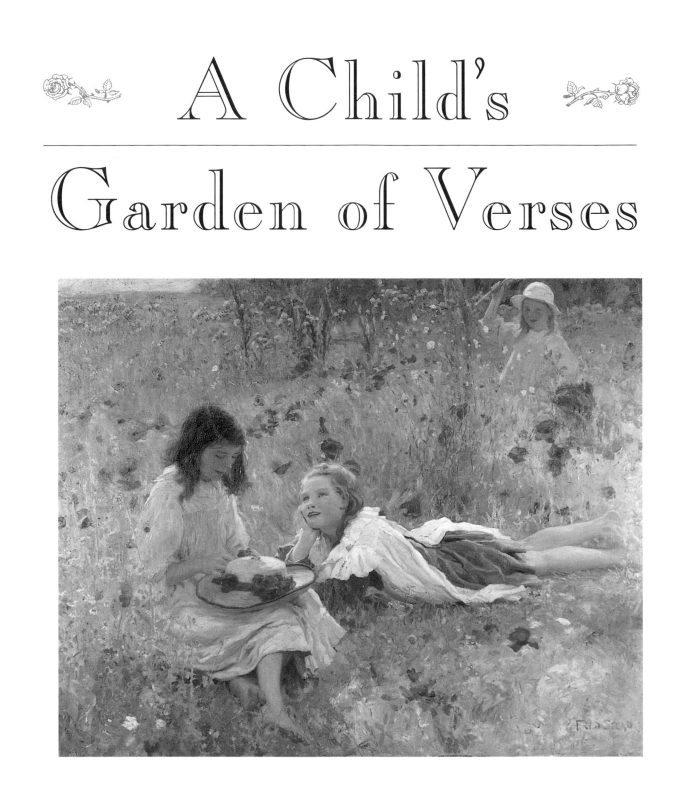

ROBERT LOUIS STEVENSON

DK PUBLISHING, INC.

A Child's
Garden of Verses

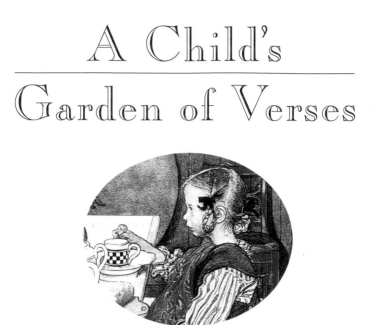

INTRODUCTION

A Child's Garden of Verses was written by Robert Louis Stevenson between 1881 and 1884, when he was in his thirties. As he told his nurse, Alison Cunningham, this "ragged little regiment" of poems was about his own childhood and was dedicated to her, "who did so much to make that happy."

There is nothing else quite like the poems in the English language. Childhood thoughts, pleasures, and fancies are expressed in a child's voice as vividly as a child experiences them. The wonderfully chosen words, rhythms, and rhymes have delighted generations of young readers, who return to the poems in adulthood as a sunny reminder of innocent days.

This book is a selection of the poems that are most appropriate today. The paintings evoke scenes of childhood as brilliantly as the words. They show children intent on play in beautiful canvases of garden, meadow, and sea. They are impressions of color and light that follow the poems through the seasons of the changing year. This is a marvelous introduction to poetry and to painting.

CONTENTS

The Wind

I SAW you toss the kites on high
And blow the birds about the sky;
And all around I heard you pass,
Like ladies' skirts across the grass –
    O wind, a-blowing all day long,
    O wind, that sings so loud a song!

I saw the different things you did,
But always you yourself you hid.
I felt you push, I heard you call,
I could not see yourself at all –
    O wind, a-blowing all day long,
    O wind, that sings so loud a song!

O you that are so strong and cold,
O blower, are you young or old?
Are you a beast of field and tree,
Or just a stronger child than me?
    O wind, a-blowing all day long,
    O wind, that sings so loud a song!

Edgard Wiethase (1881–1965), *The Kite*

The Cow

THE friendly cow, all red and white,
    I love with all my heart:
She gives me cream with all her might,
    To eat with apple-tart.

She wanders lowing here and there,
    And yet she cannot stray,
All in the pleasant open air,
    The pleasant light of day;

And blown by all the winds that pass
    And wet with all the showers,
She walks among the meadow grass
    And eats the meadow flowers.

R.H. Brock (fl. 1890), *Calves in Springtime*

The Flowers

ALL the names I know from nurse:
Gardener's garters, Shepherd's purse,
Bachelor's buttons, Lady's smock,
And the Lady Hollyhock.

Fairy places, fairy things,
Fairy woods where the wild bee wings,
Tiny trees for tiny dames –
These must all be fairy names!

Tiny woods below whose boughs
Shady fairies weave a house;
Tiny tree-tops, rose or thyme,
Where the braver fairies climb!

Fair are grown-up people's trees,
But the fairest woods are these;
Where if I were not so tall,
I should live for good and all.

Albrecht Dürer (1471–1528), *Great Piece of Turf – Study of Weeds*

Summer Sun

GREAT is the sun, and wide he goes
Through empty heaven without repose;
And in the blue and glowing days
More thick than rain he showers his rays.

Though closer still the blinds we pull
To keep the shady parlour cool,
Yet he will find a chink or two
To slip his golden fingers through.

The dusty attic, spider-clad,
He, through the keyhole, maketh glad;
And through the broken edge of tiles,
Into the laddered hayloft smiles.

Meantime his golden face around
He bares to all the garden ground,
And sheds a warm and glittering look
Among the ivy's inmost nook.

Above the hills, along the blue
Round the bright air with footing true.
To please the child, to paint the rose,
The gardener of the World, he goes.

Fred Stead (b.1863), *Poppies*

The Swing

How do you like to go up in a swing,
     Up in the air so blue?
Oh, I do think it the pleasantest thing
     Ever a child can do!

Up in the air and over the wall,
     Till I can see so wide,
Rivers and trees and cattle and all
     Over the countryside -

Till I look down on the garden green,
     Down on the roof so brown -
Up in the air I go flying again,
     Up in the air and down!

William Heath Robinson (1872–1944), *The Swing Moves,* from *The Snow Queen*

At the Seaside

WHEN I was down beside the sea
A wooden spade they gave to me
    To dig the sandy shore.
My holes were empty like a cup,
In every hole the sea came up,
    Till it could come no more.

Frans Smeers (1873–1960), *Collecting Shells*

From a Railway Carriage

Faster than fairies, faster than witches,
Bridges and houses, hedges and ditches;
And charging along like troops in a battle,
All through the meadows the horses and cattle:
All of the sights of the hill and the plain
Fly as thick as driving rain;
And ever again, in the wink of an eye,
Painted stations whistle by.

Here is a child who clambers and scrambles,
All by himself and gathering brambles;
Here is a tramp who stands and gazes;
And there is the green for stringing the daisies!
Here is a cart run away in the road
Lumping along with man and load;
And here is a mill and there is a river:
Each a glimpse and gone for ever!

Derold Page (Living artist), *Late Summer Landscape*

Derold Page 1979

Where Go the Boats?

Dark brown is the river,
 Golden is the sand.
It flows along for ever,
 With trees on either hand.

Green leaves a-floating,
 Castles of the foam,
Boats of mine a-boating –
 Where will all come home?

On goes the river
 And out past the mill,
Away down the valley,
 Away down the hill.

Away down the river,
 A hundred miles or more,
Other little children
 Shall bring my boats ashore.

Francis Danby (1793-1861), *Boy Sailing a Little Boat*

Rain

THe rain is raining all around,
    It falls on field and tree,
It rains on the umbrellas here,
    And on the ships at sea.

Maxime Maufra (1861–1918), *La Pluie, Quai de Concarneau*

Winter-time

Late lies the wintry sun a-bed,
A frosty, fiery sleepy-head;
Blinks but an hour or two; and then,
A blood-red orange, sets again.

Before the stars have left the skies,
At morning in the dark I rise;
And shivering in my nakedness,
By the cold candle, bathe and dress.

Close by the jolly fire I sit
To warm my frozen bones a bit;
Or with a reindeer-sled, explore
The colder countries round the door.

When, to go out, my nurse doth wrap
Me in my comforter and cap:
The cold wind burns my face, and blows
Its frosty pepper up my nose.

Black are my steps on silver sod;
Thick blows my frosty breath abroad;
And tree and house, and hill and lake,
Are frosted like a wedding-cake.

Bernard Frohlich (b. 1823), *Children in the Snow*

Picture-books in Winter

SUMMER fading, winter comes –
Frosty mornings, tingling thumbs,
Window robins, winter rooks,
And the picture story-books.

Water now is turned to stone
Nurse and I can walk upon;
Still we find the flowing brooks
In the picture story-books.

All the pretty things put by,
Wait upon the children's eye,
Sheep and shepherds, trees and crooks,
In the picture story-books.

We may see how all things are,
Seas and cities, near and far,
And the flying fairies' looks,
In the picture story-books.

How am I to sing your praise,
Happy chimney-corner days,
Sitting safe in nursery nooks,
Reading picture story-books?

Adelaide Claxton (fl. 1860-76), *Wonderland*

Whole Duty of Children

A CHILD should always say what's true,
And speak when he is spoken to,
And behave mannerly at table;
At least as far as he is able.

Carl Larsson (1853–1919), *Lisbeth at Table*

To Any Reader

As FROM the house your mother sees
You playing round the garden trees
So you may see, if you will look
Through the windows of this book,
Another child, far, far away,
And in another garden, play.
But do not think you can at all,
By knocking on the window, call
That child to hear you. He intent
Is all on his play-business bent.
He does not hear; he will not look,
Nor yet be lured out of his book.
For, long ago, the truth to say,
He has grown up and gone away,
And it is but a child of air
That lingers in the garden there.

Claude Monet (1840–1926), *The Artist's House at Argenteuil*

Carl Larsson (1853–1919), *In the Holly Hedge*